REWILD the World at BEDTIME

REWILD the World at BEDTIME

written by
Emily Hawkins

illustrated by
Ella Beech

WIDE EYED EDITIONS

Contents

Rewilding Our World

As we listen to the news about our planet warming up, and wildlife disappearing, it's natural to feel worried. Over the past few centuries, human actions have had a powerful impact on the world, causing problems for plants and animals, as well as for people. Nowadays, many wild places are at risk, and many creatures are in danger. But despite this, **it's important to remember that there are lots of reasons to be hopeful.**

Inside this book, you'll discover twenty stories about real-life projects from across the globe that are "rewilding" the world in different ways. So what exactly is rewilding? It's an attempt to **undo the damage**; to **bring wildlife back** to the places where it once thrived. Sometimes, it involves lending a helping hand to restore plants and animals to a particular area; **sometimes, it involves stepping back and allowing nature to heal itself.**

As you will see, rewilding can help repair our world in many ways, from **reducing floods and wildfires** to **reversing animal extinctions** and **tackling climate change**. It's an opportunity to restore the rich diversity of the natural world; to weave the complex, beautiful tapestry of life back together.

Through these stories you can travel the globe, finding out about the incredible work being done to **help nature recover.** From small British farms to the vast American prairies, from the bamboo forests of China to the African savannah, you will meet astonishing animals and extraordinary people who are working to protect them. We'd like to think that you'll **be inspired by these true tales**—by the resilience of the wildlife, and by the remarkable dedication of the people trying to mend the mistakes of the past... and give us all **hope for the future**.

Going Wild on the Farm
Knepp Wildland, England

Once, in a small corner of Sussex in the south of England, there lived a pair of farmers named Charlie and Isabella. They worked hard to make a living. Like most farmers, they plowed their fields to prepare the soil for planting, they put up fences to stop their animals from roaming too far, and across the landscape they sprayed chemicals—lots of chemicals. Some to help the crops grow, some to kill the weeds, and some to get rid of the bugs who ate the crops.

But despite all this work, it was a struggle to make any money. First of all, the chemicals and the farm machinery were expensive. Secondly, the soil on the farm was impossible. In the winter, the thick, claggy clay was hopelessly waterlogged, while in summer it dried out, becoming parched and unyielding. It was hard to grow enough to keep the farm going. Every day, a new bill would land on the doormat, and the debts piled up. Charlie and Isabella didn't know what to do.

What would happen, they thought, if they stopped fighting against nature?

But one day, they hit upon a plan. Charlie had been reading a book by a Dutch scientist who had some new ideas about how to manage landscapes. What would happen, they thought, if they stopped fighting against nature? If they took their hands off the steering wheel and let the wild take over? They decided to find out. But first, they had work to do.

To start with, they sold the farm machinery and the dairy cows. Then, they tore out the fencing—miles and miles of wires and posts that had neatly divided one field from another. Next, they dug up all the old drains: instead of forcing the rainwater to follow a certain route, they would let it lie where it wanted to.

Going Wild on the Farm

They scattered wildflower seeds, and introduced some new animals to the farm...

They brought in a herd of longhorn cattle and allowed them to wander wherever they wished. They welcomed Tamworth pigs: long-snouted snufflers who delved and foraged, feasting on fallen acorns and nutritious roots. Then came fallow deer, red deer, and roe deer, and a troop of sturdy little Exmoor ponies, robust enough to withstand harsh winters. The creatures were encouraged to roam freely across the landscape, grazing on grasses, browsing on shrubs and trees.

Once, the farm had been a dull, muddy place, with few flowers, birds, or bugs. The chemicals that had showered the fields had killed the wild plants and bugs that the birds and other animals needed to eat. But soon, things started to change. Without the constant churning of the plow, the ground no longer turned to mud, and the grazing creatures that ambled here and there began to alter the landscape.

The cattle wove among the trees, their hefty bodies making clearings for sunlight to shine through. As they lumbered around, they left steaming cowpats behind them—dollops of rich fertilizer crammed with hundreds of seeds, ready to grow.

Roe deer

Fallow deer

Exmoor pony

Tamworth pig

Red deer

Longhorn cow

The pigs rummaged through the undergrowth, and exposed patches of bare earth where these seeds could take root. Before long, the farm was unrecognizable. Where once the land had been covered in fields of the same crops, in neat rows, now there was an untamed tangle of woodland and wildflower meadows, scrublands and marshes, ponds and streams, and a riot of wildlife.

Without chemicals, the bugs flourished. The pastures and hedgerows were abuzz with bees and beetles, while purple emperor butterflies flitted among the oak canopies, and meadow browns, marbled whites, and tortoiseshells fluttered low over the shrublands. Attracted by the wild abundance, some rare species of bat moved in, as well as harvest mice, water shrews, bank voles, and hedgehogs.

Now there were plentiful seeds and bugs to eat, many wild birds returned. Soon, the precious calls of turtle doves and nightingales could be heard as they nested among the hawthorn and honeysuckle. Woodpeckers and cuckoos roosted in the trees, while woodcocks and little egrets waded in the wetlands. Kingfishers darted above ponds and rivers—startling flashes of blue that streaked across the sky.

Among the grassy glades bounded rabbits, which attracted falcons, goshawks, red kites, and sparrowhawks. Little owls and barn owls could be seen, along with tawny owls, short-eared owls, and long-eared owls—in fact, every one of the five types of British owl could be found here. It was spectacular!

Charlie and Isabella couldn't believe it—nature was thriving in a way they had never thought possible. As well as providing a new home for many rare types of wildlife, their farm attracted people who came to enjoy the beautiful surroundings and camp in the wildflower meadows, shepherd's huts, and treehouses. They made enough money from the farm shop and the campers to keep things running smoothly—in fact, they were better off than before. And every year, they were astonished and delighted by the surprises nature had in store: from swimming pigs to basking butterflies. It seemed that once they stepped back and let nature take its course, marvelous things could happen.

Rewilding the Rivers
Nijmegen, The Netherlands

Once, upon the banks of a river, there stood a city. This city had been there for two thousand years, since the ancient days of the Romans. Beside it, the flowing waters carried people and goods to and fro, allowing the city to grow and prosper. But the river also carried something else: the ever-present risk of danger.

To the east of the city of Nijmegen, the wide channel narrowed suddenly and turned a sharp corner, forming a pinch point. When the rain was heavy, people worried that the river might burst its banks and flood the city. To protect themselves, they had built huge barriers, called dikes, along the shoreline, holding the waters back. But thirty years ago, the rain was stronger than ever, swelling the river until it threatened to spill over the dikes and surge across the city.

Rewilding the Rivers

Thousands of people were forced to leave their homes and travel to safety.

Fortunately, the dikes held firm and, once the waters subsided, the people could return. But this brush with disaster made them worry. What if next time they weren't so lucky? What could they do to avoid the worst? Some believed that the dikes needed to be built taller and stronger than before. But others had a different idea: what if instead of barriers, the river was given more space? What if it was allowed to follow its natural course? What if the dikes were taken down, and rebuilt further inland, allowing the river to spread across a wide flood plain?

To begin with, it was difficult to persuade everyone to agree to the plan.

To begin with, it was difficult to persuade everyone to agree to the plan. Giving the river more room meant moving farms and homes, which wasn't popular. And who would pay for it all?

First of all, the planners designed a clever scheme: as well as building new homes in safer places, they would construct a new bridge across the river, making it easier for the people to get around, which helped convince them to support the changes.

Then, the planners had another smart idea. They knew that the riverbanks held a thick layer of clay and sand, which had built up over the centuries and was valuable for making bricks. So they asked the brickmaking companies to help pay for the project in return for taking the sand and gravel to use in their factories.

Over the next twenty-five years, the project team bought up land along the shoreline opposite the city. The dikes were taken down and rebuilt several hundred feet inland, giving the river much more space to flow and flood naturally. The brick companies removed the silts and clays from the old flood plain, while repairing and restoring the riverbed, creating extra channels for the flood waters.

Then, it was time for the wildlife to move in. Herds of wild horses and cattle were introduced—hardy grazers that roved across the flood plain, munching on meadow sage and thistles, spreading seeds in their poop and encouraging plants to grow. When the rains were heavy, these plants helped slow down and soak up the water,

reducing the risk of flooding further downstream. In winter and spring, when the river rose and spread out, the animals could move to higher ground, returning to the lower meadows once the waters receded.

The landscape slowly changed: woodlands appeared, as well as flowering grasslands, islands, marshes, lakes, and drifting dunes. With these new habitats came more creatures: beavers and badgers, black terns and bluethroats, skylarks, spoonbills, and storks.

Now, along the banks of one of Europe's busiest rivers, was a beautiful wilderness. The people of the city enjoyed exploring this new natural playground on their doorstep: they walked and ran, cycled and sunbathed, while watching the wildlife all around them. It seemed that the planners had solved the problem of flooding at the same time as creating a new wild place where both animals and people could roam free. Their idea—of rewilding the riverbanks, of working with nature instead of fighting against it—soon spread to other cities, and to other countries around the world. By giving the river more space, everyone benefited.

The Missing Lynx
Iberian Peninsula

Dusk. **The gentle chorus of cicadas pulses through the warm air. As the shadows lengthen and the sky darkens, a slender shape slinks across the sandy scrubland. Lynx.**

Many years ago, thousands of these graceful cats prowled the grasslands of Spain and Portugal. But life became hard for the Iberian lynx. Slowly, as human settlements and farms sprawled outward, and roads reached their tarmac tendrils across the landscape, the wild habitats of the lynx began to vanish.

They were hunted for their fur, and some landowners saw them as pests. Until the 1950s, the Spanish government even rewarded people for killing these cats. With their numbers falling, just when it seemed things couldn't get much worse for the lynx, another disaster befell them.

A deadly virus started to spread among European rabbits, the lynx's favorite food. An Iberian lynx must catch one a day to sustain itself. If it has young cubs to feed, it needs even more. So when the virus all but wiped out the local rabbits, the lynxes were in deep trouble.

By the turn of the century, things were looking bleak. The Iberian lynx had become the rarest cat in the world, with fewer than one hundred thought to exist in the wild. Drastic action was needed, but what could be done?

The Missing Lynx

The Spanish and Portuguese governments, together with scientists and wildlife charities, launched a project to breed cubs in captivity. The team rescued several young lynxes who had little chance of surviving on their own. They hoped these cats would go on to have babies, but there was no guarantee. Would the captured lynxes settle into their new home? It was all very uncertain.

The team hoped that one day, the cubs could be set free.

However, in 2005, there was a happy arrival. The first cubs—three beautiful bundles of fluff—were born in the breeding center to their mother, Saliega. The team hoped that one day, the cubs could be set free. But before this could happen, there was a lot to do...

First, the lynxes needed a safe habitat to be released into. In some parts of Spain and Portugal, people had been leaving the countryside in large numbers, abandoning their homes and farms, moving to the cities to find work. For the lynx, this was good news. Conservation teams began to buy up areas of land, ripe for rewilding.

This land was in a bad state. Once, it had been grazed by farm animals, but with the animals gone there was nothing to keep the plants under control. A thick blanket of dry bushes now covered the landscape, raising the risk of catastrophic wildfires that could tear across huge areas. Something needed to change.

The project teams brought in herds of wild grazers—horses, wild boar, and roe deer. Between them, they began to repair and restore the countryside in a gentle way. They moved slowly, chewing and chomping, nibbling and gnawing as they went. After a while, their grazing created a patchwork of open pastures among the dense scrub, which not only acted as natural firebreaks, but also provided the perfect habitat for lynxes.

But the landscape wasn't quite ready for the lynxes yet. One of the major threats to their safety was road traffic, so the teams set about building underpasses to help the creatures navigate highways. They also installed speed bumps and traffic lights, warning drivers to slow down.

Other problems to overcome included changing the way farmers felt toward the lynx, as well as ensuring there was enough prey for them to eat. Thankfully, the number of rabbits began to recover, helped by efforts from the project teams. They also worked hard to show landowners that lynxes could be useful. These reclusive cats rarely killed farm animals. In fact, they hunt the foxes that prey on sheep, so they could be seen by farmers as helpful friends.

In 2010, the first captive-born cubs were released into the wild, followed by many more over the next few years. The results were remarkable. While in 2002 there had been fewer than one hundred lynx in the wild, now there are more than one thousand. There is still work to do, however: the project teams plan to expand the lynx's range even further, and create corridors of rabbit-rich wilderness so the cats can travel safely between different regions.

The Missing Lynx

This majestic feline, with its tufted ears and distinguished whiskers, has made an extraordinary comeback. The triumph of the project shows what can be accomplished when people pull together and work hand in hand with nature to achieve a goal. It also shows just how resilient the natural world is: when it's given the chance to recover and thrive, miraculous things are possible.

The Water-Buffalo Whisperer

Ukraine

Once there was a young man named Michel, who lived among the green and beautiful mountains of western Ukraine. As a boy, growing up in Germany, he had always been fascinated by animals. After studying forestry at university, he traveled around Europe, volunteering on small farms, trying to find a way of life that didn't harm the natural world.

One day, while he was hiking in Ukraine's Carpathian Mountains, he came across a herd of goats, in the middle of which was a surprising animal—a water buffalo! Michel was confused: he thought that water buffalo only lived in Asia—what was this one doing here?

He learned that these beasts had lived in the region for over 1,500 years, helping farmers by pulling their plows and giving them milk. But recently, he discovered, these creatures were dying out. As the number of small farms dwindled, and large dairy farms became common, people no longer wanted to keep buffaloes, who had a reputation for being aggressive and difficult to milk. In fact, there were fewer than one hundred Carpathian water buffaloes left.

So, he decided to help. He moved to the mountains and began to learn the local language and traditional way of life. He traveled from farm to farm, rescuing unwanted buffaloes. A few village leaders gave him some land for grazing his herd, and he built a wooden cabin in the foothills, where he lived a simple life.

Michel spent many hours with his herd, getting to know their personalities. He was patient and kind with them, and over time, these clever, sensitive animals came to trust him. They produced rich, creamy milk that he could use to make yogurt and cheese.

As the years passed, Michel's herd grew. Each morning, sitting astride one of his buffalo friends, he would guide the creatures up to the high meadows to feed upon the lush pastures, returning to the lower slopes as dusk fell. He became famous as an expert on these rare and special animals. People across Europe began to hear about Michel and his herd. Which is why, when a team of rewilders began searching for hefty herbivores to graze a river habitat in the Danube Delta, in southern Ukraine, they got in touch with Michel. They needed his buffaloes!

Rewild the World at Bedtime

The landscape in question was Ermakov Island, at the mouth of the Danube River. A few years before, the dikes and dams that had surrounded the island had been removed, meaning that life-bringing seasonal floods could once again wash over the land, as they had done in the past.

Leaf cutter bees

Cormorant

The project team were on the lookout for a herd of water buffalo, who could move to the island as landscape engineers, helping to restore the area and bring back its wildlife. Michel agreed to donate seventeen of his buffaloes to the project. He traveled with them in May 2019, on the long journey by truck and barge.

Almost as soon as the buffaloes disembarked, they began to transform their new home, grazing, trampling, and wallowing. They were the ideal residents for this soggy region, perfectly at home in their swampy surroundings. They roamed around, spreading seeds as they went, which were carried in their heavy fur or deposited in their poop.

As the buffaloes explored, they began to open up the densely packed reed beds, creating puddles and pools. Before long, these new habitats became home to smaller creatures: bugs, fish, red-bellied toads, and marsh frogs. This new life attracted pelicans and herons, storks and terns. Just by being themselves, Michel's buffaloes brought rich diversity to the area.

Today, Michel still tends the rest of his herd among the wild foothills of the Carpathian Mountains. Surrounded by alpine meadows, green pastures, orchards, and oak forests, he teaches people about ways of farming that don't harm the environment. And he believes that with the help of the animals, we can repair many landscapes, allowing the natural world to heal itself.

Heron

Pelicans

Bringing Back the Beaver

River Otter, England

As the light fades and dusk descends on the valley, the scents of water mint and meadowsweet mingle in the air. Beside the river, all is still. Then—plop!—the plump body of a beaver slides into the stream, her proud nose twitching above the surface as her feet paddle beneath. She has a busy evening ahead—sticks to gather and a dam to build—but the twinkle in her dark eyes suggests everything is under control. She arches her back and ducks below the water, heading for the bankside tunnel that leads to the woodland. Her night's work is about to begin.

Once, the sight of a beaver bustling about its business was common across Europe. But sadly, these plucky plant-eaters were nearly wiped out by humans, who hunted them for their meat and their soft, warm fur. As marshlands were drained and farms spread out, many watery habitats were lost, and by about three hundred years ago beavers had completely disappeared from Britain, with only a handful clinging on in the rest of Europe.

But these bewhiskered beasts were missed. They are famous for transforming landscapes with their building skills. To make a home, called a lodge, they first create a deep pool of water, where they will be safe from predators. To do this, they gnaw through tree branches with their huge front teeth. They lay the branches across a stream to create a dam, forcing the water to spread out and deepen. Once a pool appears, the beavers pile up sticks and mud in the middle to make their cosy lodge, where they snuggle up safely with their babies, called kits.

But the dams, lodges, and pools built by busy paws don't only benefit beavers... they breathe life into the whole landscape and help wildlife to blossom. Beaver dams provide habitats for many plants and bugs, which in turn attract fish and water voles, otters and birds. With the help of beavers, small streams can be transformed into flourishing wetlands.

And so, about thirty years ago, wildlife experts in Britain decided to bring the beavers back.

Across the channel in Europe these characterful creatures had been restored to many rivers—surely it was time for them to return to the waterways of Britain, too?

But things were not straightforward. Some people didn't want the beavers to return. They were so used to living without them they couldn't imagine how they would fit back in. Farmers said that the bothersome beavers would cause damage and flood their fields. Fishermen said their dams would make trouble for salmon, blocking their path as they tried to travel upstream. The quarrelling dragged on for years!

Tom suspected that beavers might be at work... but how could he be sure?

One day, a wildlife-lover named Tom, who lived in Devon, spotted some peculiar goings-on down by the banks of the River Otter, near his home. He noticed that a few tree stumps had been gnawed to pencil-like points, with telltale tooth marks. Tom suspected that beavers might be at work... but how could he be sure?

That evening, he set up a night-vision camera to record any creatures that might be moving about in the darkness. Then, he waited. The next morning, he was delighted to find that his camera had captured something—a family of beavers playing happily in the water!

News of the river's furry residents soon spread far and wide, and many people were thrilled. But nobody knew where the beavers had come from. Some thought that they might have escaped from a local nature reserve; others wondered whether they'd been secretly released by wildlife activists known as "beaver bombers."

However they'd got there, the beavers seemed to be making themselves very much at home on the riverbank. But some local landowners were worried. They thought that the new arrivals might damage their property and spread disease. Fishing organizations were not happy. They believed that these large rodents might harm the fish—so they complained to the government, saying that the troublesome newcomers ought to be removed.

The government announced that the beavers would be rounded up and taken to a zoo, where they would live in captivity. But they had underestimated something very important: many people loved their new neighbors. Even the farmer who owned the land where the beavers were living wanted them to stay!

Everyone sprang into action. Meetings were held, petitions were signed, letters were written, money was raised, and "Save Our Beavers" posters were stuck up all over the area. Children dressed up in beaver costumes, planned assemblies, and sang songs to rally support. But the government were still not sure whether to allow the beavers to stay... their fate hung in the balance.

Then, one night, there was a terrible storm. The unrelenting rain fell in sheets. It poured and poured. The people who lived near the mouth of the river prepared themselves: their houses had flooded many times before, and they assumed the same would happen again. They set to work, piling up sandbags to keep out the water and expecting the worst.

But in the morning, their homes were still dry. The river had not burst its banks.

They had underestimated something very important: many people loved their new neighbors.

The flood hadn't come! Why not? How could they explain this lucky turn of events? The answer, of course, was the presence of their new neighbors... the beavers!

Scientists have proven that in places where beavers are living, flooding is much less common. Beavers can dramatically alter how fast a river flows: their dams slow down the surge of water, holding it back, so areas downstream are protected in heavy rainfall. In fact, habitats with beaver dams hold about ten times more water than those without. As well as reducing floods and helping wildlife by creating beautiful wetlands, beaver dams and lodges also clean the water, filtering out chemicals and pollution.

Eventually, the government admitted that the beavers had earned their right to stay. They were good for wildlife, they were good for water quality, and they were good for people, reducing flooding in towns and villages.

Bringing Back the Beaver

Some farmers were still worried about the impact the beavers might have, but by working with wildlife experts, they came up with solutions. For example, in places where beaver dams and pools were causing problems, special pipes called "beaver deceivers" could be installed to help lower the water levels and protect the fields. In other places, beavers might be moved to habitats that were more suitable for them, away from land where crops were being grown.

When Tom first captured his film of the beaver family, he had no idea of the challenges that lay ahead. But today, there are communities of beavers living wild in both Scotland and England, and these gentle herbivores have been made a protected species. Sometimes, just by doing what comes naturally, a single creature has the power to solve a whole host of problems.

The Song of the Humpback Whale

Sapphire Coast, Australia

As the sun rises high above the wide ocean, a small boat sets out from shore. It is packed with tourists, keen for a glimpse of a mighty humpback whale. They line up at the railings, eagle-eyed, cameras at the ready. This region is known as the Humpback Highway: every year, it sees thousands of whales pass through on their long journey south to the icy waters of the Antarctic.

The watchers don't have long to wait. A shower of brine erupts from the surface, then a long, tapered fin appears, pointing skyward. The crowd gasp, they clap, they hold their breath. They watch, wide-eyed, as the huge body of a whale leaps from the water, a glistening wall of black, rising, twisting, falling. Splash!

Soon, this mother and her playful pod will move on, continuing their journey south. Let's dive into the ocean and follow close behind...

As the whales swim, flying through the water, they call to each other, singing haunting melodies that travel many miles beneath the waves. If we could understand their songs, what would we learn? Perhaps we would hear them sing sad stories of the past, of the time not so long ago when their ancestors were hunted by humans for their meat and the oil from their blubber. During these dark years, many thousands of whales were killed, until only a few hundred humpbacks remained.

But fortunately, things have changed. In the 1980s, whale-hunting was banned across most of the globe. Today, the number of whales traveling up and down Australia's coastline has bounced back: there are now thought to be about 40,000 humpbacks that pass through these waters every year.

Stay close. Follow. Dive... down through the dark waters, down into the deep. As the whale plunges lower, she opens her cavernous mouth, scooping in small fish and clouds of tiny krill.

After eating her fill, she surges upward, muscular tail thrusting toward the surface. There, she releases a great plume of manure that spreads out in her wake: an immense bloom of nutrient-laden, life-giving poop! This rich fertilizer feeds the forests of plankton that grow in the ocean, which absorb carbon from the atmosphere and give out oxygen. Land creatures, like us humans, owe every other breath we take to the plants of the sea, and also to the whales— the gardeners of the ocean—who help them grow.

The Song of the Humpback Whale

Remarkably, whale manure powers the whole marine food chain. Thanks to these blooms of fertilizer, the flourishing plankton feed vast shoals of krill that sustain not only the whales, but multitudes of other creatures. When a whale dies, it sinks to the seabed, taking with it the carbon that the plankton removed from the air. This is how the mighty whale pump works: because of these colossal beasts, who move gracefully up and down through the blue-black layers of the ocean, nutrients are brought to the surface, and carbon is locked away in the inky depths. It turns out that these gentle giants of the sea are also giants in the fight against climate change.

We can't keep up with them for long. Eventually, the pod moves beyond us, out of reach, their wide tail flukes rising and falling, each sleek back arcing elegantly through the waves.

We watch them go, and are thankful—thankful that these remarkable creatures are thriving once again, thankful for the vital role they play in the ocean's great circle of life, and thankful for all they do to help repair and restore our beautiful planet.

The Return of the Elephants

Gorongosa National Park, Mozambique

As the red sun drops toward the horizon, a herd of elephants gather by a lake, their reflections mirrored in the calm water. On the far side of the pool, a jeep approaches across the dusty savannah. The driver is a young woman called Dominique: a scientist whose job is to learn about and protect these majestic beasts. She switches off the engine and reaches for her binoculars.

Dominique watches as the leader of the herd flaps her ears, raises her trunk, and lets out a bellow of alarm. This wise mother elephant is protective of her family, and is wary of people. She has a long memory. She remembers a time not so many years ago when this place, Gorongosa, was a battleground.

The Return of the Elephants

In the 1960s, Gorongosa National Park thrummed with wildlife. People came from across the globe to gaze at lions and leopards, rhinos and elephants. This vast landscape was a paradise of lush green flood plains, grassy savannahs, wetlands, woodlands, and mountains.

When the war finally ended, the park was unrecognizable.

But then, a dark shadow fell across the land. In the 1970s, the country of Mozambique was torn apart by a devastating civil war, which raged for sixteen years. The fighting spread into the park as the land was claimed first by one side, then the other. The war took a toll on the wildlife. Zebra and wildebeest were hunted for their meat, while elephants were killed for their valuable tusks, which were sold to buy weapons and supplies.

When the war finally ended, the park was unrecognizable. Roads had been destroyed, buildings had been reduced to rubble, and the ground was littered with the bones of lost creatures. Most of Gorongosa's large animals had died.

Where once there had been more than two thousand elephants, now there were fewer than two hundred. The buffalo had vanished, and the rhinos, leopards, and lions had been wiped out. The landscape had changed too. Without the grazing animals, the grasses had grown tall and a thorny shrub had taken hold, sprawling across the plains in dense thickets.

But now that the fighting was over, both the people and the wildlife could begin to heal. The managers of the park tried to unite the local community, hiring ex-soldiers from both sides of the war as park rangers. They patrolled the savannahs, scaring off poachers and removing the deadly traps and snares left behind. Nature breathed a sigh of relief and, gradually, the wildlife began to return. However, the recovery was slow and the park was short of money to fix its problems.

In 2004, an American businessman called Greg Carr visited Mozambique. He had made a fortune in computer software, and he wanted to give back to a good cause. Greg fell in love with Gorongosa, and invested millions of dollars in helping the park recover. With his support, the park had enough money not only to bring back the animals, but also to build schools and provide healthcare and jobs for the people who lived in and around Gorongosa.

Over the next few years, many different plants and animals returned to the area, and scientists were hired to research these varied species. One of the new staff was Dominique. She had been born in the nearby city of Beira just as the war was ending. She'd grown up with a love of science, and had studied ecology and conservation at university. When Dominique heard about the exciting work taking place at Gorongosa, she knew that she had to be part of it. She landed a job on the scientific team, and she is now an expert on the park's elephants.

The Return of the Elephants

These mighty creatures are crucial to Gorongosa's recovery. With their lumbering bodies and powerful trunks, they transform landscapes. As a herd passes through, they munch on tall grasses and chomp at thorny shrubs, making space for antelopes and other grazers. But, as Dominique would learn, although the elephant population is recovering, there are still challenges to face. Part of her job is to find ways for humans and elephants to live alongside each other happily.

Sometimes these creatures come into conflict with the people who live nearby. On Gorongosa's southern border is a river that the elephants occasionally cross, visiting farms to raid and trample the crops. To solve this problem, staff and local people put up fences made from roped-together beehives to protect the farms. If the elephants disturb the fence, the bees become agitated and sting them, until they back off. These clever hives, as well as keeping the elephants away, provide the farmers with honey to eat and sell. Projects like this, where both the wildlife and the human communities benefit, are vital to Gorongosa.

Today, as Dominique watches the herd cooling off at the lake, she is filled with hope for the future. In the thirty years that have passed since Mozambique's civil war ended, much has changed for the better. Wildlife populations in Gorongosa have rebounded, local people are happier, and this vibrant place is now home to a breathtaking variety of animals and plants, as well as a close-knit community of people who are dedicated to taking care of them.

Pleistocene Park
Siberia, Russia

Many thousands of years ago, in the frozen north, herds of huge, hairy herbivores patrolled the land. The woolly mammoths lived at the end of the Pleistocene Epoch, which we also call the Ice Age. As these massive creatures roamed, they grazed and trampled, using their powerful tusks to uproot trees and dig under the snow for shrubs and grasses to eat. All this stomping and rootling changed the landscape, making space for smaller animals and plants to thrive.

At this time, much of the far north was covered in grasslands, thanks, in part, to the mammoths, who kept the area clear and open. Deep beneath these grasslands extended a layer of cold earth, the permafrost, which stayed frozen all year round. But about twelve thousand years ago, the mammoths began to die out until, eventually, they vanished altogether. What killed them? Did these plodding giants at last surrender to the freezing temperatures of the Ice Age, or were they the victims of a new, more deadly, threat... humans?

Sadly, scientists believe that early humans may have hunted the mammoths and many other large Ice Age creatures to extinction.

After the mammoths and the other big beasts disappeared, the landscape transformed again. Now there were no hefty herbivores to tend the grasslands, a blanket of cold, wet moss took hold, spreading across regions that we now call the tundra. Elsewhere, dense forests sprang up, which stand to this day. But beneath them, underground, the thick layer of permafrost remained, locking in the frozen traces of plants and animals from thousands of years before.

In the 1980s a Russian scientist named Sergey moved to the northeast of Siberia, to study the permafrost. Along the banks of a river, he found ancient bones that had been revealed by a crumbling cliff. By examining them, he learned that this cold and empty landscape had once been home to an astonishing number of creatures: mammoths, bison, wild horses, woolly rhinos, reindeer, lions, and wolves. He realized this region had once been a sweeping grassland: a colder version of the African savannah, supporting a similar variety of creatures.

Sergey also discovered something worrying: because of climate change, the permafrost had begun to melt, which risked releasing lots of greenhouse gases into the atmosphere—gases that would warm the planet even more. But Sergey had an idea. What if the ancient grasslands of thousands of years ago could be restored? What if the animals could be brought back?

It would be tough to replace the extinct mammoths, but perhaps bison, reindeer, and musk ox might do a similar job, keeping the grasslands open and free from moss and trees?

Sergey wondered if the light-colored grassland would absorb less heat than the dark moss, and so slow down the melting of the permafrost. In the 1990s he set up an exciting new project, which he called Pleistocene Park. He fenced off a large area of land and arranged to bring in herds of grazing animals. Moving the creatures to their new home, however, was not an easy job. The park lies in one of the most remote parts of the world, across which the animals had to be transported by icy road and river barge. But gradually, over the years, Sergey and his son Nikita have managed to bring many creatures to the park, including wild horses, elk, musk ox, reindeer, a herd of bison, and even woolly camels.

As these heavy-footed beasts have spread across the landscape, grazing and delving, they have broken up the spongy layer of moss covering the ground, allowing the grasslands to flourish. Although the harsh conditions bring many challenges, Sergey and Nikita have shown that, with the help of the animals, the vast expanses of the far north can be transformed.

Pleistocene Park

Meanwhile, on the other side of the world, at Harvard University in the USA, a team of scientists are working on a project that could one day help Sergey and Nikita fulfil their dream. They plan to use new technologies to reinvent the woolly mammoth! They are hoping that by combining mammoth DNA found in fossils with the DNA of Asian elephants, they can create a new type of furry elephant that's hardy enough to withstand the temperatures of Siberia.

Perhaps, in the future, herds of grazing mammoths will once again roam the snowy plains of the far north, doing their bit to guard against global warming. Until then, Sergey and Nikita plan to keep up their work, spurred on by their vision that one day, this wilderness will throng with life once again, just as it did thousands of years ago.

The Wolves of Yellowstone Park

USA

This is a story about wolves. You'll have heard stories about wolves before: big, bad wolves that gobble up people and animals. You might think that by banishing wolves from a landscape, the rest of the wildlife would be better off. But it's not as simple as that, as the rangers of the oldest national park in the United States would discover...

Long ago, the mournful howl of the gray wolf was a common sound across much of North America. Living wild and free, the wolf packs ranged through the forests and mountains of this rugged, beautiful continent for thousands of years.

To protect the spectacular beauty of America's landscape, Yellowstone Park was created in 1872. It was the world's first national park, and it stretched across a vast area of Wyoming, Montana, and Idaho. With its majestic mountains and craggy canyons, tumbling waterfalls and crystal-clear lakes, the dramatic landscapes of Yellowstone were rich in wildlife.

The wolves fed on the park's elk and deer, playing an important part in keeping the numbers of grazing plant-eaters in check. But these predators, with their watchful amber eyes and sharp-toothed jaws, made some people nervous. Farmers and ranchers, in particular, hated the wolves—they feared that these clever hunters would prey on their livestock. In the first half of the last century, thousands of wolves were killed across North America.

One day, in 1926, a Yellowstone ranger shot the park's last wolf. In that moment, everything changed for the wildlife of Yellowstone... but nobody predicted the consequences. Now that the wolves had gone, the elk, newly bold, ventured out of the forests.

In that moment, everything changed for the wildlife of Yellowstone... but nobody predicted the consequences.

They began to gather in large herds, grazing the grassy valleys and crowding along the riverbanks. They nibbled at the trees and trampled young saplings. The growing herds ate so many plants that the riversides were almost bare.

Without the trees' roots twining firmly through the earth, the riverbanks began to crumble away. And without plants to feed on, many other creatures now had nothing to eat. The beavers and otters began to disappear. The frogs and fish vanished. The songbirds flew away.

In the absence of the wolves, the coyotes were the top dogs. They hunted baby antelopes, rabbits and mice. Fewer small animals meant there was less food around for the other predators—the hawks and the weasels, the foxes and the badgers.

As the wildlife faded away, people started to think differently about what wolves could do for a landscape. By the 1970s, the people in charge of Yellowstone had decided they needed to bring the wolves back. But there was a long road ahead. Cattle ranchers were worried that the wolves would kill their animals, and some locals feared they might even attack people.

The Wolves of Yellowstone Park

After twenty years of planning and preparing, the day finally arrived. On a snowy morning in January 1995, crowds of people gathered to welcome some new arrivals to the park. At last, a trailer carrying a crate came into view: the wolves of Yellowstone were back!

This group of fourteen wolves had been brought all the way from Canada, from a landscape of mountains and meadows similar to Yellowstone's. They had been carefully chosen in the hope that they would soon get used to their new home—but nobody knew for sure if they would stick around. The year after these first wolves were released, they were joined by more new arrivals. The creatures formed packs and settled in. They were here to stay.

This might seem unfair on the elk, who had become used to life without predators. While the slow and the weak would fall prey to the wolves, on the whole the herds were better off. Their numbers could return to a healthy level, and plants could recover, leaving enough food for everyone.

Almost as soon as the wolves arrived, the landscape started to change. The deer and elk began avoiding the valleys where they might be trapped, so the riverbanks returned to life. As the aspens and willows took hold again, the songbirds came back. The beavers returned, and the wetlands they built created homes for otters, muskrats, fish, and water birds. The wolves scared off the coyotes, meaning that the pronghorn antelopes could thrive again, and numbers of gophers, rabbits, and mice increased, providing food for hungry birds of prey. Even scavengers such as bears and cougars were better off, now they could feast on the remains left behind by the wolf packs. It seemed that bringing back the wolves was the key to rebuilding the broken strands of Yellowstone's web of life.

Today, more than twenty five years since the wolves returned, there are now at least eight different packs that roam the wilds of Yellowstone. On a still evening, if you pause by the misty shores of a lake, you might be lucky enough to hear the howl of a wolf in the distance, claiming its territory. The wolves of Yellowstone are home at last.

The Return of the Sea Otters
British Columbia, Canada

In the gray-green waters off the western shores of Canada, there once grew a vast forest on the seabed. From the rocky floor sprouted ribbons of seaweed, called kelp, reaching long fingers up toward the light.

In among these swaying strands lived many types of creature. Swarms of shrimp drifted between the trailing tendrils, while crabs scuttled in and out of the rocky crevices. Purple sea urchins with needle-sharp spines crept along the seabed, while shoals of fish—greenling and rockfish, kelpfish and mackerel—darted to and fro, seeking shelter among the drifting leaves.

Watching over it all were the playful lords of the forest: the sea otters. These clever creatures, with their fluffy bodies and grizzled faces, bobbed at the surface, dozing and grooming, before diving down to hunt for urchins, crabs, and clams. In these chilly waters the otters needed lots of food—a quarter of their body weight every day—to keep up their strength.

For many years the forest thrived, its plants and creatures linked together in a web of life. The sea urchins ate the kelp, but the otters ate the sea urchins, protecting the forest and keeping it healthy. The indigenous people lived alongside the otters, and the waters held enough shellfish for everyone to have a generous share.

But then, everything changed. When European settlers arrived in North America, they began to hunt the otters for their thick, warm fur, which was shipped abroad to be sold. Before the fur-traders arrived, there had been hundreds of thousands of otters. But by the end of the 1800s, there were only about two thousand left. On a sad day in 1929, the last sea otter in Canadian waters was killed in the waters off Vancouver Island.

With the otters gone, there was nobody to keep the hordes of hungry sea urchins under control. These prickly critters laid their eggs, which hatched into new urchins, which, in turn, made more urchins. Soon, the greedy guzzlers had formed a huge army. They rampaged across the ocean floor, gorging on seagrass and mowing down kelp. Before long, huge swathes of greenery had been destroyed, many creatures had lost their food and shelter, and only the urchins remained.

The forest that had once towered beneath the waves was gone.

Slowly, the people began to understand what they had done: that by removing the otters, they had changed so much more than they at first realized. But fortunately, it wasn't too late. Far to the west, in the cold waters of Alaska, a few otters had survived the fur-hunters.

In 1969, a plane took off from a remote Alaskan island carrying a very unusual cargo... otters! These whiskery passengers had been carefully captured in nets by skilled fishermen, then loaded into special crates for the voyage.

Rewild the World at Bedtime

After a long flight over the north Pacific, they were released into the waters of a quiet bay on the west of Vancouver Island.

More flights followed over the next few years, until eighty-nine otters altogether had made the journey from Alaska to Canada. But, after being snatched away so suddenly from their old homes, would the otters settle in to their new ones? The people waited, and hoped.

They didn't have to wait long. It soon became clear that the otters were very happy. In the sheltered bays and inlets of the island, they quickly made themselves at home. They had babies and moved further afield, spreading out along the coastline. Now the otters were back, they feasted on the sea urchins, meaning that the kelp forest could rise again. And with the return of the forest came the return of all the other creatures that had once found food and shelter among its rippling fronds: shellfish and starfish, seals and sea lions, fish and octopus.

In the sheltered bays and inlets of the island, they quickly made themselves at home.

The remarkable recovery of the ocean forest, and its lovable guardians, reminds us that even when things look bleak, the natural world might just have the power to heal itself, if we let it—especially with a little help from its furry friends.

Panda School
Sichuan Province, China

In the rustling bamboo groves that cling to the mountainsides of central China live some of the world's most endearing animals: giant pandas. These black-and-white bears, with their plump bodies and fluffy faces, spend up to fourteen hours each day feasting on bamboo. They need to eat about 45 pounds of the stuff every day to survive!

Long ago, the pandas had a huge territory in which to roam, ranging across a vast area of south and eastern China. Sometimes, the bamboo plants in their forest homes would die off, but the bears could always move to a neighboring mountainside to find more food. However, when people began to spread across the landscape with their farms and their factories, slicing up the wilderness with roads and railways, the pandas suffered. Many forests were cut down, and the bears were hunted for their thick, valuable fur.

The pandas found themselves pushed back by human settlements, their wild homes disappearing. At the end of the 1970s, giant pandas existed in only a tiny fraction of their old territory, in six isolated mountain ranges in central China. In the 1980s, much of the bamboo in these forests died, which meant that the pandas, with nowhere to go, died too. Soon, there were only about one thousand giant pandas left in the wild.

Panda School

As often happens, the people were slow to notice the damage they had done. But when they realized that these beloved bears might soon be gone forever, they began a huge effort to save them. First of all, hunting pandas was banned—anyone caught poaching them could face twenty years in prison. Secondly, the government worked with wildlife charities to create nature reserves where cutting down trees became illegal.

But because these habitats were broken up and scattered—separated from each other by roads and farms—it was difficult for the bears to find mates and have babies. Even though their forest homes were now protected, the future of the giant panda remained uncertain. So then came the next part of the plan: a panda-breeding project the likes of which had never been seen! Scientists set up breeding centers where they hoped that captive bears would have cubs, which could be released into the wild.

It was a long and difficult process. For the pandas, life in captivity was very different from life in the wild, and for a while the bears didn't seem interested in mating or having babies. But over many years, the scientists who studied the pandas got better at learning how to help them have cubs, and how to care for the cubs once they'd been born. These days, there are dozens—in fact hundreds—of adorable baby pandas in the breeding centers, and the next part of the job is to prepare them for life in the wild.

To survive on their own, the baby pandas need to learn to be wary of other animals, including humans, which means that the youngsters shouldn't get too attached to their human keepers. The keepers disguise themselves as pandas, dressing up in panda costumes whenever they interact with the cubs. They don't just have to look the part—they also have to smell just right, so the costumes are sprayed with panda pee to conceal their human scent!

When a cub who has been chosen for release is about a year old, it moves with its mother to a large enclosure on a forested mountainside, similar to a wild habitat. Here, the pair are free to roam around, and the mother teaches the cub to find food and water.

Panda School

Inside the fence there are no leopards or other predators, but the youngster must learn to fear these creatures if it is to survive in the wild. Before it can be released, it must be ready to face danger. In place of a real leopard the keepers bring a stuffed one into the enclosure, which has been rubbed with leopard droppings so it smells real. The keepers stay out of sight while they wait to see how the youngster will react. When the cub approaches, it sees the stuffed leopard, it smells its scent, and it hears a recording of a leopard growling. With luck, the panda will be afraid and will scramble away to safety. If so, it has passed the test!

Finally, once a cub is two years old and has learned to fend for itself and to recognize danger, it is ready to be set free. But not all the cubs raised in captivity can or will be released—only a small number of them have been trained for survival in this way.

Today, the numbers of giant pandas are slowly creeping back up. In the 1980s there were only about one thousand pandas in the wild; today there are closer to two thousand. The Chinese government have announced the launch of the Giant Panda National Park, which will link together existing nature reserves so these precious bears can rove across a larger, more connected, area.

Before it can be released, it must be ready to face danger.

There is still much work to do to restore the bamboo forests where the pandas roam, in order to help them and the other creatures that live alongside them. But the efforts of the past few decades have shown what can be achieved when people work together to repair the damage they have done. For the giant pandas of China, the future is looking hopeful.

Slow and Steady
Mauritius, Indian Ocean

Y ou've probably heard of the dodo. This plump, flightless bird once lived peacefully on the island of Mauritius, until it died out a few hundred years ago. The dodo is the most famous extinct creature from Mauritius—but sadly, it's not the only one...

This jewel of an island, with its white sandy beaches and turquoise waters, lies in the Indian Ocean, off the eastern shores of Africa. Like many islands, it once had a unique collection of wildlife, which developed over thousands of years, cut off from the rest of the world. Mauritius was home not only to dodos, but also to giant tortoises. These enormous reptiles, who could live for more than one hundred years, spent their days plodding around, nibbling on shrubs, and browsing on low-hanging fruits.

There were no predators on Mauritius or its surrounding islands, so the tortoises got comfortable, never needing to fear other creatures. But this meant that when European seafarers arrived in the 1600s, the defenseless, trusting plant-eaters didn't stand a chance.

Unfortunately for the tortoises, the sailors found them tasty to eat—tragically tasty. They captured these slow-moving beasts in their hundreds, bundling them onto ships to provide fresh meat on long voyages. To make matters worse, the sailors also brought other animals to the islands—cats and dogs, rats and rabbits, pigs and goats—who quickly made themselves at home. The pigs and rats feasted on the tortoises' eggs, while the cats ate the hatchlings and the goats and rabbits devoured their favorite plants. Before long, the giant tortoises of Mauritius had died out altogether, going the same way as the dodo.

The loss of these gentle creatures meant trouble for the rest of the wildlife. Like elephants and other large herbivores, giant tortoises do an important job in shaping their habitats, by grazing on plants and spreading seeds for new growth. When the tortoises disappeared, the plants became less rich and varied, which was bad news for the bugs and birds who depended on them for food and homes. The lives of the islands' plants and animals were so closely entwined and delicately balanced that when one part was removed, everything else came crashing down, like a house of cards.

But there was still hope.

Pink pigeon

Mauritius kestrel

Echo parakeet

Mauritius olive white-eye

Ornate day gecko

- 58 -

In 1984 the Mauritian Wildlife Foundation (MWF) was set up, and the team embarked on a project to restore the wildlife of two small islands: Isle aux Aigrettes, which lies off the southeast coast of Mauritius, and Round Island, which lies to the northeast.

To restore the islands' wildlife, they started by removing the rats, cats, rabbits, and goats. With these troublesome newcomers gone, at first things began to improve for the other creatures—for the kestrels and parakeets, the golden bats and pink pigeons. But then the team realized that by removing the grazing rabbits and goats, they had made it easy for a fast-spreading tall weed to grow out of control, pushing out the grasses and shrubs that were native to the islands. Some sort of large plant-eater—a replacement for the giant tortoises that had died out—was needed to solve the problem. But which creature would be best?

Helping the project team was a British biologist named Carl Jones, who worked for the Durrell Wildlife Conservation Trust. When he was a boy, growing up in the Welsh countryside, he used to rescue injured animals, caring for them in his garden until he had nursed them back to health. As a young man, he moved to Mauritius to help save the endangered Mauritius kestrel. And when he weighed up the situation on the islands, he had an idea.

Slow and Steady

Carl suggested that to replace the giant tortoises that had died out, they could use a closely related giant tortoise from the Aldabra Islands, some 60 miles away to the northwest. At first, people didn't like the plan. They pointed out that a lot of effort had just been made to get rid the non-native animals from the islands—wasn't it silly to bring in another new species? But Carl argued that if they didn't do something, the islands' native plants and animals would disappear forever. The situation was desperate.

Eventually, Carl and the MWF team won people round. After all, they said, if things didn't work, it would be easy to capture the tortoises, because they moved so slowly! And so, about twenty years ago, a few groups of Aldabra giant tortoises were brought to the islands. To begin with they were kept in large enclosures while they settled in, but after a few years they were allowed to roam free. There are now more than six hundred tortoises on Round Island.

Now that giant tortoises have returned, much of the other wildlife is bouncing back.

This trusty crew of grazing gardeners are doing brilliant work. The placid plodders have eaten up the tall weeds, making space for the other plants to recover. The tortoises feed on the succulent fruits of the endangered ebony tree, scattering the seeds in their dung, so the seedlings can take root far and wide. Now that giant tortoises have returned, much of the other wildlife is bouncing back, including many endangered species of birds and reptiles.

Thanks in part to the tortoises, and the nature-lovers who fought for them, the wildlife of these islands is slowly recovering. With his hands-on approach, Carl showed that by helping one species, we can also help a whole range of other creatures. There is always something we can do to make a difference—and there is always a place for hope.

Rewilding the Great Plains
Montana, USA

Big skies. Endless grasslands stretching to the horizon. A herd of majestic bison, their hulking silhouettes black against the skyline. Welcome to the Great Plains.

The North American Great Plains are a huge expanse of grassland lying between the Mississippi River in the east and the Rocky Mountains in the west. Once, this vast landscape teemed with wildlife: pronghorn and elk grazed the lush grasses, while wolves and foxes prowled through the undergrowth. Prairie dogs burrowed beneath the ground, while golden eagles hovered in the skies above. Across the rolling prairies roamed herds of bison, kicking up clouds of dust as they thundered past. The people, in general, lived in harmony with nature, seeing themselves as part of the natural world, instead of ruling over it.

But sadly, as is often the story, when European settlers arrived on the scene, the wildlife suffered. In the 1800s, as the settlers spread west across North America, they tamed the wilderness.

The rich grasslands were plowed and tilled, fenced and divided, and the bison—also called buffalo—were hunted in their millions. Within a century, these beasts had nearly disappeared.

But all was not lost. Even though the wild animals of the prairie lands had been pushed to the fringes, they clung on in remote places. And this meant that with a bit of effort, they could be brought back to their original habitats.

Today, in the state of Montana, there are many groups trying to rewild these ancient grasslands. The Aaniiih and Nakoda peoples of the Fort Belknap Indian Reservation are leading the way in restoring lost wildlife. In the 1970s they welcomed the first group of bison back to their tribal pastures, and this herd is now nearly one thousand strong. They have also reintroduced other endangered prairie-dwellers, such as the swift fox and the black-footed ferret.

In the year 2001, a group of wildlife-lovers set up the American Prairie Foundation, with a mission to create an enormous, open area of wilderness. They raised money to buy up pieces of private land, linking together existing nature reserves— a bit like filling in the missing pieces of a jigsaw puzzle. They removed the fences separating these parcels of land, allowing the animals to roam freely. So far, the American Prairie Reserve has stitched together more than 450,000 acres—an area more than twice the size of New York City—but their great hope is to expand the reserve to more than 3 million acres: roughly the same size as the US state of Connecticut, or Northern Ireland in the UK. This huge rewilding project has big ambitions—as big as the far-reaching skies of Montana itself.

In the past twenty years, more and more bison have been brought back to the prairies. These massive beasts are powerful landscape engineers, able to create beautifully diverse habitats, just by doing what comes naturally. Bison love to wallow in the dirt, which helps remove ticks and fleas from their shaggy coats. They paw at the earth with their hooves, and scrape away the turf with their horns, making wallows to roll around in. From these dusty holes in the ground, small marvels appear. When it rains, the wallows collect water, transforming into little wetlands that support many forms of life—bugs, birds, chorus frogs, and spadefoot toads.

As the grazing herds roam across the landscape, they leave grasses of different heights, providing perfect habitats for prairie birds: thick-billed longspurs and Sprague's pipits; grasshopper sparrows and lark buntings. In their wake, the bison deposit steaming piles of dung, which provide nutrients for plants, and homes for hundreds of different types of bugs.

Rewilding the Great Plains

But bison aren't the only creatures helping to shape the landscape and support the wildlife of the Great Plains. The humble prairie dog also does an important job. These burrowing rodents live in underground colonies. As they dig through the earth, they create safe shelters for other species—such as burrowing owls—which depend on the prairie dogs to survive.

Prairie dogs play a vital role in the food chain because they are preyed upon by badgers, coyotes, eagles, hawks, and the rare black-footed ferret. The little tunnelers were once seen as pests by ranchers, and were nearly wiped out—but projects like American Prairie are doing their best to protect them.

Rewilding the Great Plains is important not only to protect animals, but also to help tackle climate change. The prairies—these vast oceans of grass—can soak up large amounts of carbon dioxide, locking it away in the soil to help slow down global warming.

Nowadays, on the grasslands of Montana, you can see soaring eagles and thundering herds of bison, and you can hear the howling of coyotes, just like long ago. People come to hike and to cycle, to bird-watch and to camp under the wide starry skies, marveling at the beauty of this ancient landscape. On the American prairies, there are many reasons to be hopeful.

Saving the Tigers

Nepal

As dawn breaks in the jungle, a thin veil of mist hangs over the still river. Padding toward the water on silent paws, a tiger appears from the tall grass, its fur the color of flame, its amber eyes ringed with black. Combining grace and power, beauty and danger, it's no wonder this magnificent beast has always inspired both awe and fear in humankind.

In 1900, there were roughly one hundred thousand tigers living in the wild. But as the years passed and humans spread out, tigers' territories were encroached upon and hemmed in. They were hunted to make tiger-skin rugs and tiger-bone wine; their teeth and claws were sold to make jewelery and lucky charms. By 2010, only about three thousand remained. And so began the battle to bring the largest cats in the world back from the brink of extinction.

In the foothills of the Himalayan Mountains, the lush, green lowlands of Nepal are home to many endangered creatures, including rhinos and elephants—but in 2009 a survey counted

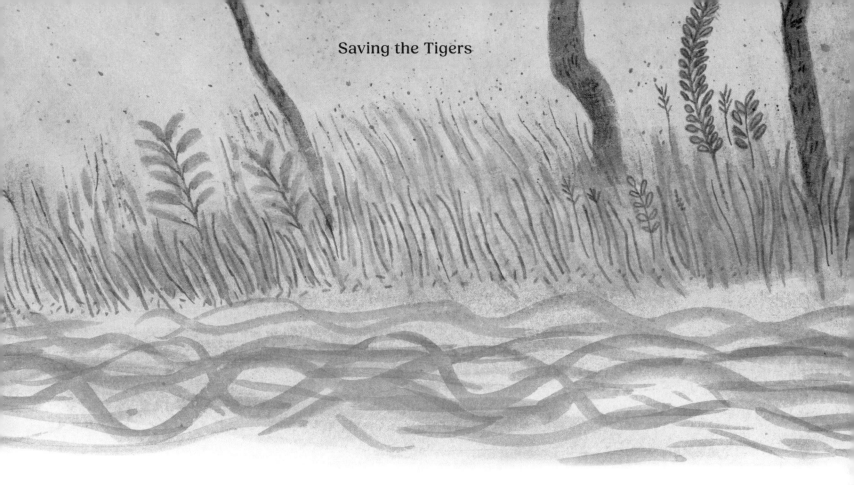

only 122 tigers. Since then, the Nepalese people have worked tirelessly to protect these rare creatures and their precious habitats.

Firstly, the wild places where tigers live were expanded, forests were restored, and national parks were set up where hunting was illegal. The governments of Nepal and its neighbor, India, worked to create safe wildlife corridors, so tigers could roam freely between regions.

Next, there was a huge effort to stamp out poaching in Nepal. From the lofty backs of elephants, soldiers patrolled the forests to arrest anyone trying to harm the tigers. They used drones, surveillance cameras, and dectection dogs to help them in their work, and in 2011 not a single tiger was killed by poachers in the forests of Nepal.

But there was a problem: where people and predators live close together, trouble is never far away. As the number of tigers increased, so too did the conflicts between these big cats and their human neighbors. Sometimes the tigers killed the people's cows or goats; sometimes the people themselves were killed. Despite wanting to protect these special creatures, many local communities were living in fear.

New fences were built to protect people and farm animals, and villagers were compensated if their animals were attacked by tigers. Many tourists began visiting to see the wildlife, which brought jobs and money to the area, helping the local people. Children were taught about the dangers of wandering alone in the forest, and what to do if they came face to face with a tiger. But despite these attempts to reduce the clashes between tigers and humans, there wasn't a simple answer to the problem.

Many women still traveled into the forest every day to collect firewood. This meant that not only were lots of trees were being cut down, but the women risked running into their dangerous, sharp-toothed neighbors.

However, since 2007 the wildlife charity WWF has been helping to bring new biogas stoves to thousands of homes in the area. Instead of using wood for fuel, they use animal dung. These clever stoves give off less carbon dioxide than woodstoves, so they are better for the environment, and they emit less harmful smoke, so they are better for people's health, too. They also result in fewer trips to the forest—saving trees, saving people, and saving tigers!

Thanks to all of these efforts, the tigers of Nepal have made an impressive recovery.

Saving the Tigers

In 2022 there was a huge survey—thousands of cameras were set up to take photos as the animals passed by, and the pictures were used to count up the big cats based on their unique patterns of stripes.

The numbers revealed that there are now 355 tigers living wild in Nepal—more than twice as many as in 2009. There is still work to do to help people and tigers live peacefully side by side, but these results show what is possible for tigers everywhere. One day soon, these remarkable creatures may be the kings of the Asian jungle once again, just as they were long ago.

Saving the Monarch Butterflies

North America

Each year in the skies above North America, an astonishing natural event takes place. As the days get shorter and winter approaches, clouds of monarch butterflies leave their summer breeding grounds in Canada and the United States to begin their long journey south. These delicate creatures travel thousands of miles, navigating by the light of the sun, crossing mountains and rivers, braving storms and high winds. Eventually, the tiny travelers arrive in southern California or central Mexico, where they gather in forest groves, crowding together on swaying branches, blanketing the trees with their flame-colored wings.

At the end of winter, the females head north again, laying their eggs on milkweed plants along the way. When the stripy caterpillars hatch, they gorge on the milkweed leaves, eating constantly for about two weeks. Then, each caterpillar transforms into a chrysalis before emerging as a vibrant butterfly—and so the cycle of life continues.

These iconic bugs have been making this epic migration for centuries. Once, they flocked in their millions. But now, they are in danger. In 2020, only a few thousand western monarchs were counted in California, and the eastern monarchs are in trouble too.

There are several reasons for this. Firstly, many wild habitats have been lost, so the butterflies have fewer places to rest and feed during their long journeys. Secondly, because of the powerful weed killers used by farmers, the number of milkweed plants has plummeted, so when the hungry caterpillars hatch they have nothing to eat. Climate change, too, means that the monarchs have to contend with extreme weather, such as hurricanes and droughts, as they travel.

Saving the Monarch Butterflies

But it's not too late to save these beloved butterflies. Thousands of people are trying to help. Conservation groups, biologists, and volunteers are battling to rescue the monarch from the edge of extinction. School children and scout troops are planting milkweed to feed the caterpillars. Gardeners and farmers are sowing milkweed too, along with other nectar-rich plants to feed the adults. In the state parks of California, staff are growing eucalyptus trees, which the monarchs love to roost in during the winter. In towns and cities, local mayors are making a pledge, promising to create welcoming habitats for these well-loved bugs. All across America—along roadsides and rivers, in fields and meadows, in backyards and city gardens—people are taking action.

All across America —along roadsides and rivers, in fields and meadows, in backyards and city gardens— people are taking action.

Every November in California, hundreds of volunteers set out, armed with binoculars, to count the monarchs as they roost and, lately, their numbers seem to be creeping back up again. The battle to save these orange-and-black beauties is far from over, but there is hope that everyone's efforts will pay off. Butterfly-lovers have faith that these winged wonders will bounce back, continuing their spectacular migrations for centuries to come.

Wet and Wild

Iberá Wetlands, Argentina

On a rainy January night in 2021, something important happened in Iberá Park. Three jaguars—Mariua and her cubs—took their first steps into the wild. As they padded out of their enclosure, these graceful cats made history: they were the first jaguars to roam this landscape for seventy years. Bringing back missing animals to their natural habitats is not quick or easy. The story of Mariua and her cubs, and of Iberá Park itself, started many years before.

Iberá, which means "shining waters" in the language of the Guaraní people, is a vast wetland in northeast Argentina: a blue-and-green patchwork of pools, streams, and islands. Sadly, over the past few centuries, the actions of humans changed this landscape, and many animals lost their homes. As cattle ranching boomed in Argentina, the wildlife of the wetland disappeared: the jaguars vanished; the red-and-green macaws flew away; the giant anteaters died out. One day in 1997, a plane touched down in Iberá. On board were a North American couple called Doug and Kris Tompkins. They had made their fortunes in the business of outdoor clothing, and now they wanted to spend their money on the natural world. They were hoping to create a new nature reserve. At first, Kris wasn't impressed by this swampy region: it was hot, sticky, and swarming with mosquitoes. But Doug had other ideas. He saw beauty in the landscape, and a month later he went back and bought a large piece of the wetland.

At the time, an increase in floods in the area meant that many local ranchers were selling their land. As each new parcel of property came up for sale, the Tompkins bought it. To start with, some people were suspicious of these wealthy foreigners—why did they need so much land? What were they planning to do with it? Many rumors swirled.

But over time, attitudes toward the couple softened as their purpose became clear: they wanted to turn the wetland into a national park, bringing back lost species. They convinced people that the project would benefit not only the natural world, but also local businesses, by creating jobs and attracting tourists. And they brought in a team of Argentinian wildlife experts to help make this vision a reality.

The first animals to be released back into the landscape were the giant anteaters. The project team began rescuing young, orphaned anteaters whose mothers had been killed by hunters elsewhere in Argentina. To begin, just one pair were set free in the wetlands, but today, the park is home to hundreds of these long-nosed, bushy-tailed beasts.

> The project would benefit not only the natural world, but also local businesses, by creating jobs and attracting tourists.

Anteater

Pampas deer

Next came the endangered pampas deer, which now bound neatly across the grasslands. Then, it was the turn of the collared peccaries: busy-snouted grazers, similar to pigs, who rootle for fruits, spreading seeds across the landscape. Small groups of peccaries were released into the park, and they happily spread out and multiplied.

The biggest challenge was bringing back the red-and-green macaw, which hadn't flown wild in Argentina since the 1800s. The team collected the parrots from zoos and wildlife centers, but because they had been bred in captivity, they hadn't developed proper flight muscles. Before they could be released, the birds had to be taught not only how to find food and recognize predators, but also how to fly! It was a tricky process, but at last thirteen macaws were ready to be set free. Soon, the park celebrated the hatching of the first wild macaw chicks in over one hundred years.

Red-and-green macaw

Collared peccary

The most headline-grabbing new arrivals were the jaguars. The project crew had worried that their cattle-ranching neighbors might not be keen on the return of these predators. But people were very supportive—after all, jaguars had always been important to the Guaraní culture. The team were new to the business of big-cat rewilding, so they asked advice from experts in Africa. They opened a jaguar breeding center, welcoming captive big cats in the hope that their cubs could one day be released into the wild.

Capybara

And that day finally came in 2021, when Mariua and her little ones walked free. Since then, eight more jaguars have been released, and nine cubs have been born in the wild. As the jaguars increase in number, they will hunt capybara and other large plant-eaters, keeping the grazing creatures in check to ensure a healthy balance between animals and plants.

Eventually, all the wetlands that had been bought by the Tompkins were given to the Argentinian government, helping to create Great Iberá Park, Argentina's largest natural park. It provides many jobs for local people, who work as wildlife rangers and tour guides, taking visitors on kayak tours and horseback treks. Today in Iberá, caimans lurk among the lily pads while kingfishers dive for fish; marsh deer tread gently through the still waters while capybara graze along the shores. In this beautiful wetland, day by day, nature is slowly recovering.

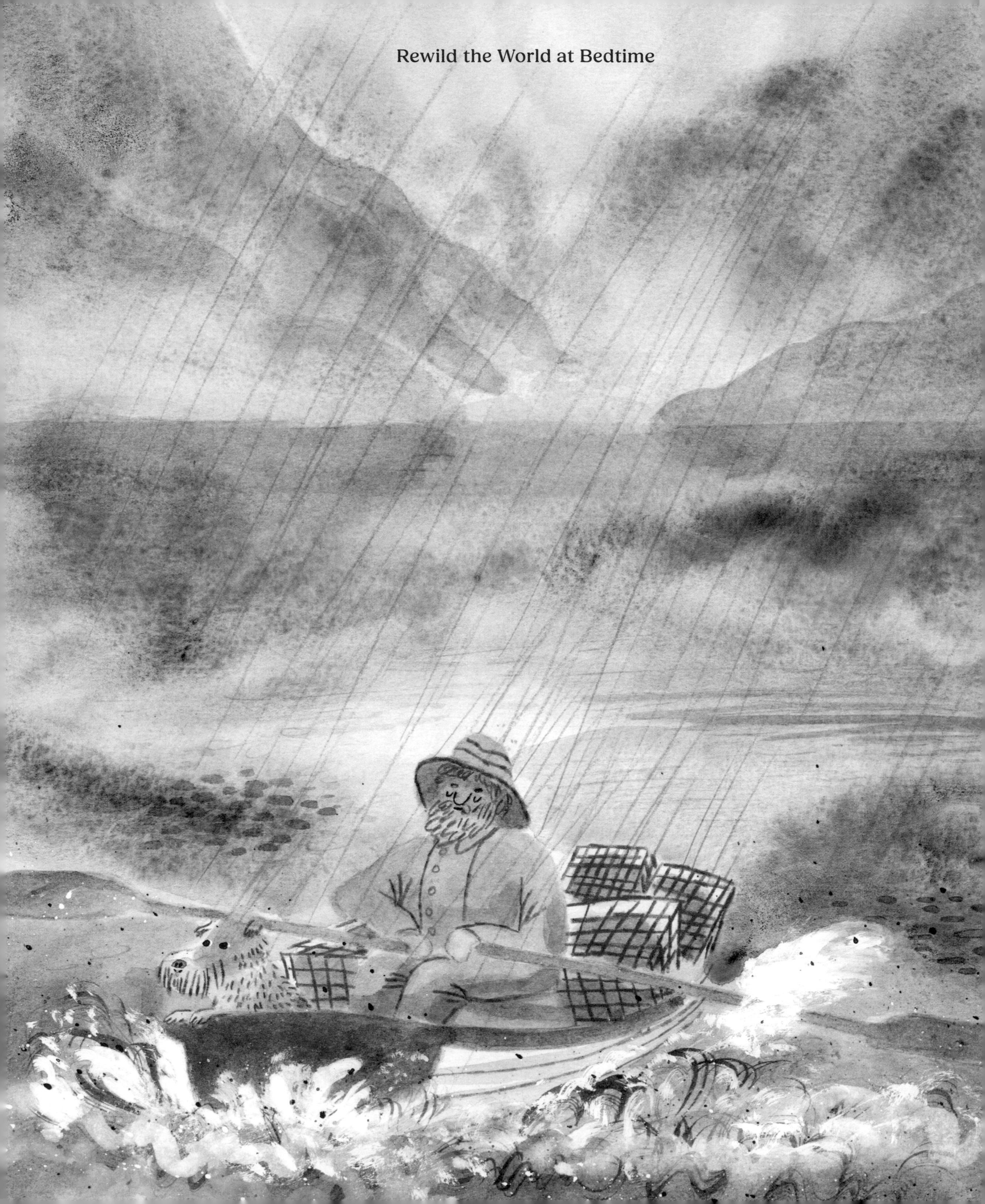

The Great Kākāpō Rescue

New Zealand

One day in 1896, a small boat set out onto the choppy waters of Dusky Sound, New Zealand. Hunched over the oars was a lone man, his face lined and weather-beaten, his beard streaked with gray. As the wind swelled and the waves crashed over the sides, the man rowed on. He carried a special cargo: a collection of cages, each sheltering a rare and precious bird.

The man was Richard Henry, and he had an important job to do: he was determined to save the kākāpō from extinction.

Kākāpō are gentle, friendly parrots that were once common in New Zealand. These remarkable birds—the world's heaviest parrots—are astonishingly ancient.

They have existed on these islands for thirty million years. For most of this time, they lived in peace, undisturbed by predators. There were no fierce mammals to chase the birds, so they didn't need to take to the air—they became flightless, spending their days waddling around or climbing trees.

But when the first humans arrived from Polynesia about 700 years ago, this spelled trouble for the kākāpō. With the settlers came dogs, which hunted the birds, and rats, which ate their eggs. The kākāpō, plump and defenseless, were easy targets.

Then, more trouble arrived with the appearance of European settlers in the early 1800s. They brought with them sheep to farm, and rabbits to hunt.

But the rabbits soon multiplied out of control, ravaging the grazing pastures. The sheep farmers decided that to solve the problem, they needed to ship over even more new creatures—stoats, weasels, and ferrets—to kill the rabbits. The release of these cunning predators meant disaster for the kākāpō.

Richard Henry—who had been born in Ireland, and had moved to New Zealand as a young man—realized that something needed to be done. He was fascinated by wildlife, and spent long days working outside. He had noticed that the kākāpō and many other native species were disappearing, and he wanted to help them.

In 1894, Richard got a new job as caretaker of Resolution Island. This wild, uninhabited place, which lay off the southwest coast of New Zealand, had just been named as a wildlife reserve. It was densely wooded and free from rats, stoats, and weasels, so it seemed the perfect place for the kākāpō. But first, Richard had to find them.

Each day he would set out with his dog, Lassie, to search for kākāpō on the mainland. Lassie, wearing a muzzle so as not to harm the birds, delved into woods and thickets to sniff them out. Richard followed the sound of Lassie's bell, gently lifting the parrots and wedging them into his backpack to carry to his cottage, keeping them safe until

it was time to make the journey across the water. When he'd collected enough birds, he would stow the crates into his boat and set off toward Resolution Island. Over four years, Lassie and Richard rescued more than five hundred kākāpō in this way.

Richard hoped that the island would be a safe haven where the native birds could thrive. But sadly, nobody at the time realized that stoats and weasels can swim. By 1900, they had invaded this sanctuary, paddling across the narrow channel to the island. Richard was devastated. It seemed he was fighting a losing battle. When Richard died at the age of 84, he believed that his mission to save the kākāpō had failed.

But his work had not been in vain. In Richard's years on Resolution Island, he'd spent a great deal of time studying and writing about his favorite birds. And the notes he made would prove hugely helpful for the wildlife-protectors of the future.

Although the kākāpō of Resolution Island didn't survive the stoat invasion, some remained in isolated parts of New Zealand.

The Great Kākāpō Rescue

In the 1980s, they were moved to several offshore islands that were out of swimming-range of predators. Today, staff on the islands work tirelessly to make sure that the birds are happy and healthy. And, many years after Richard's death, his writings on kākāpō behavior and breeding are still a vital tool in the battle to protect them.

In the early 1970s, fewer than a dozen kākāpō were known to exist, but now there are more than 250. In fact, there are so many kākāpō that scientists are looking for other homes to move them to. Resolution Island, where Richard lived for so many years, might be the answer. There are still stoats there, but a large-scale trapping effort is likely to get rid of them. In fact, New Zealand's government is hoping to make the entire country and its offshore islands free of rats and stoats by 2050. One day, perhaps the kākāpō—this beloved green parrot—might thrive on New Zealand's mainland once again, just as its ancestors did millions of years ago.

A Highway for Bees

Oslo, Norway

Once upon a time, in the northlands of Europe, a city lay nestled between sparkling blue sea on one side and forested green hills on the other. This city was the capital of Norway, a country famed for its beautiful landscapes and wildlife. The people who looked after the city did their best to make it a clean, green place, without too much pollution from cars and factories.

In the surrounding countryside, farmers and gardeners grew all sorts of crops for people to eat: potatoes and turnips, carrots and onions, strawberries, blueberries, apples, and cherries. These crops, like many others, depended on bees and other bugs to pollinate them. As the bees buzzed around, drinking nectar, they spread pollen from one flower to another, so the plants could create seeds and fruits. Without these pollinators, the plants would not grow.

But the people who lived in the city were worried. They had heard that across the world, the number of pollinators was falling. Day by day, these busy little workers were dying out. As human settlements spread across the landscape, and woods and meadows were paved over, the bees' wild homes were disappearing.

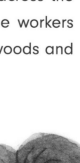

On many farms, the chemicals sprayed onto crops were harmful for bugs. The bees were in trouble.

So a group of beekeepers decided to do something about it. They realized that the bees needed more places in the city where they could rest and feed. They planned to make a Bee Highway all the way across Oslo, joining the countryside that lay north of the city with the forests to the south. This highway wasn't actually a road, but a network of flowery stopping-points scattered across the city, where the bees could find food and shelter.

The beekeepers couldn't do it alone—they needed people to help them. So they went on the news, telling everyone about the plight of the bees. They spoke to schools and businesses, city planners and local residents.

Soon, flower gardens and bug hotels were popping up on windowsills, balconies, and terraces all over town. Hotels and office blocks installed beehives on their rooftops. School children planted sunflowers, marigolds and daisies. Everybody got involved. Before long, the people had created a pollinators' passageway stretching right across the heart of the city.

The idea was so popular that it quickly spread across the world—dozens more cities followed Oslo's example.

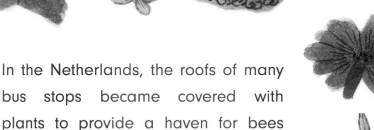

In the Netherlands, the roofs of many bus stops became covered with plants to provide a haven for bees and butterflies. In London, Paris, Washington, and Melbourne, a buzzing new world of flowers and greenery began to emerge high above the office blocks and apartments.

With their pollinators' passageway, the beekeepers of Oslo showed that when people work together, they can achieve important things. They also showed that the job of rewilding doesn't have to be done on a grand scale: you don't need thousands of acres, or heaps of money, to create change. Rewilding can happen in back gardens, on balconies, on rooftops, and bus-stops. Small steps can make a big difference.

SAVE OUR BEES!

Rewilding the Forest

Costa Rica

Once, there was a little boy called Alvaro. He lived in beautiful Costa Rica, where the forests were lush and green, and the trees were so tall they seemed to touch the sky. Alvaro loved trees. His mother and father often took him on outings to the edge of the cloud forest, where he would marvel at the ancient giants blanketed in moss and draped in vines. Sometimes, he would scramble up into the canopy and sit with his back against the trunk, watching the light through the leaves, listening for howler monkeys and the chattering of birds.

As Alvaro grew, so did his love for trees: these miracles of nature that stand between earth and sky. He learned how important they are in the battle against climate change, because they absorb huge amounts of carbon, as well as giving out oxygen for us all to breathe. He learned how they help purify the air and clean the water, as well as providing food and shelter for countless creatures.

They knew that the destruction of the forests had to be stopped... But how?

But as he grew, the forests Alvaro loved began to shrink. In Costa Rica, as in many places around the world, trees were being cut down to clear land for planting crops and farming cattle. By the time Alvaro left university, more than half of the vast forest that once covered Costa Rica had been lost. Many people were worried. They knew that the destruction of the forests had to be stopped... But how?

Alvaro had an idea. Because of his hard work and passion for nature, he had managed to impress the president of Costa Rica, who had created a new job for him: Minister of the Environment. Now, Alvaro was in a perfect position to put his plans into action.

He realized that the trees were not valued properly. In Costa Rica at that time, trees were only worth something once they had been cut down to be sold as timber. Farmers and landowners could make much more money by cutting down trees to sell wood and raise cattle than by letting the forest stand.

Alvaro had to change the way the farmers felt about the land: he had to make them see the value of trees.

But farmers trying to support their families had to be able to make money. Alvaro's idea was to pay farmers and landowners to protect and restore the forest. They were given a certain amount of money to look after the trees on their land. The scheme was hugely popular.

So where did this money come from? It doesn't grow on trees, after all! Some came from a new tax on fossil fuels; some came from foreign countries, businesses, and charities who wanted to invest in the environment. As well as paying local people to protect the forests, the government bought land to turn into national parks, and planted thousands of trees.

The results were remarkable. When Alvaro started his project, the forests had shrunk to cover only a quarter of Costa Rica; thirty years later, they stretched across more than half the country.

The once-bare hillsides began to teem with life. Toucans, green macaws, and hummingbirds flitted around the treetops, while jaguars prowled the forest floor and sloths snoozed among the branches. Tourists flocked to visit, eager to explore the jungles, cloud forests, and mangrove swamps. This created jobs for locals as tour guides and park rangers; in hotels and restaurants. And people began to feel proud of their beautiful country; proud of their precious forests.

Nowadays, Alvaro, too, is proud of the changes Costa Rica has made. By restoring its natural wonders, his country has won admiration and gratitude from around the world. And no doubt, as he sat up in the canopy many years ago, if that little boy could have seen the future, he would have been proud also—of how he would one day help to save the forests, one tree at a time.

Soaring Home to the Highlands
Scotland

Long ago, in the Highlands of Scotland, where the mist hangs low over the purple hills, wildlife once thrived. In the great Caledonian forest lived wolves and wildcats, pine martens and boars, while otters and beavers made their homes in the sparkling lochs and streams. High above it all, with their vast wings splayed like outstretched fingers, the ospreys ruled the skies. These spectacular fish-eating birds nested at the tops of ancient trees, returning year after year to raise their young.

But over time, the wild upland landscapes were tamed by humans. Across millions of acres, trees were stripped from the valley sides, making space for sheep farming. Wetlands were drained, woodlands were cut down, and wolves were hunted. As the countryside transformed and habitats were destroyed, the wildlife disappeared too. The boars, the polecats, and the elk slowly vanished.

And the ospreys—these wild wonders of the Highland skies—were killed by hunters; their eggs stolen by collectors. Slowly their numbers dwindled, until in 1916 the last nest in the British Isles lay empty, its owners never to return.

No more would they soar above the gleaming waters; no more would their shrill call be heard over the lochs and glens.

As the years passed, some people forgot about the ospreys and the other wildlife; they had grown so used to the new, bare landscapes that they didn't think about the creatures that had flourished there before. But others remembered. They waited, and they hoped, for the ospreys to return.

For nearly forty years they waited, until the 1950s, when that whistling cry was heard again. The ospreys were back! A pair traveling north for the breeding season had made their nest in a windblown pine by the shores of Loch Garten. People were delighted, and were determined to keep this precious pair safe. The Royal Society for the Protection of Birds set up Operation Osprey, where volunteers kept watch over the nest, night and day, to guard against egg thieves.

Since those days, ospreys have returned to Loch Garten to rear their chicks nearly every year. They are the region's most famous residents, attracting thousands of birders who visit every summer, eager for a glimpse of these majestic creatures. In fact, the Loch Garten eyrie is the most-watched bird's nest anywhere on the planet!

Inspired by this happy homecoming, **many people in Scotland** came together to encourage even more ospreys **back to** the Caledonian forests. Wildlife-lovers built sturdy nesting platforms at the **tops of trees** to tempt the creatures to expand their range. They guarded and **monitored** these sites, keeping the birds safe from **anyone who would harm them. And they** worked together to pass new laws, protecting the birds and their precious **eggs**. The ospreys, once thought lost from the Highlands forever, have recovered resoundingly: today, there are more than 250 breeding pairs in Scotland.

With its sweeping 5-foot wingspan, its **deadly** hooked beak, and its raking talons, the osprey is a **supreme** hunter, hovering above the **still waters** of a lake before plunging to snatch a fish. These remarkable birds fly south **every fall** to their African wintering grounds. But as spring approaches each year, Scotland's **nature-lovers** have their eyes on the horizon, waiting and watching for the arrival of the ospreys; **these** symbols of strength and resilience.

The **return** of the osprey to the Highlands **shows** how we can do things differently to allow wildlife to thrive alongside us.

The ospreys, once thought lost from the Highlands forever, have recovered resoundingly.

In Scotland today, thousands of acres of upland landscapes are being restored, and many species are recovering.

Sea eagles, goldeneye ducks, beavers, and red squirrels are on the rise, and pine martens have bounced back from the brink of extinction. As the call of the osprey echoes across the misty hills, it is a song of a triumph, of homecoming, and of hope.

Glossary

Canopy—The leafy roof of a forest.

Carbon—A natural element that, when released into the air, contributes to global warming.

Civil War—A war between different groups within the same country.

Conservation—The protection of wildlife and their habitats.

Dam—A barrier that blocks the flow of water.

Ecology—The study of living things and how they interact with their surroundings.

Extinction—When an entire species of living thing dies out.

Firebreak—A patch of cleared land that stops a fire from spreading.

Fossil fuels—Energy sources such as coal, oil, and gas made from the buried remains of ancient living things (when they are burned they release carbon into the atmosphere).

Habitat—The place where an animal or plant normally lives.

Lodge (beaver)—The home of a beaver, built out of branches.

Meadow—A field where grass and wildflowers grow.

Pasture—Grassy land grazed by animals.

Pesticide—A type of chemical designed to kill or repel bugs seen as a nuisance by farmers or gardeners.

Plankton—Tiny plants and animals that float in the oceans and are eaten by larger creatures.

Pleistocene Epoch—A period of time lasting from about 2.6 million years ago to 11,700 years ago, during which huge ice sheets covered much of the world.

Poaching—The illegal hunting of animals.

Savannah—A large grassland with scattered trees and shrubs, found near the equator.

Scrubland—An area of land covered in low-lying shrubs.

Species—A group of living things that share common characteristics and are able to interbreed.

Wetland—An area of land covered by shallow water or wet soil.

Wildlife Corridor—An area of protected land that links larger wildlife areas together, allowing animals to travel between them.

Books That Have Inspired Us

Feral: Rewilding the Land, Sea and Human Life, George Monbiot (Penguin, 2013)

Happy Stories for Nature Lovers, Dawn Casey & Domenique Serfontein (Ivy Kids, 2022)

If You Take Away the Otter, Susannah Buhrman-Deever & Matthew Trueman (Candlewick Press, 2020)

One Tree, Gretchen C. Daily & Charles J. Katz Jr. (Trinity University Press, 2018)

Rewilding: Bringing Wildlife Back Where It Belongs, David A. Steen & Chiara Fedele (Neon Squid, 2022)

Rewilding: The Radical New Science of Ecological Recovery, Paul Jepson & Cain Blythe (Icon Books, 2020)

When We Went Wild, Isabella Tree & Allira Tee (Ivy Kids, 2021)

Wilder: How Rewilding is Transforming Conservation and Changing the World, Millie Kerr (Bloomsbury Sigma, 2022)

Wilding: The Return of Nature to a British Farm, Isabella Tree (Picador, 2018)

For more information about rewilding, these organisations are a good place to start:

americanprairie.org

gorongosa.org

knepp.co.uk

news.mongabay.com

nationalgeographic.co.uk

rewildingbritain.org.uk

rewildingeurope.com

rewildingargentina.org

Acknowledgements

We are so grateful to everyone who helped bring this book to life, in particular to the inspiring people whose stories we tell. Special thanks go to Dr Andrew Digby, Dominique Gonçalves, Michel Jacobi, Carl Jones, Daniel Kinka, Dr Vikash Tatayah, Carolyn McCarthy, Sebastian di Martino, and Dr Alvaro Umaña.

Index

For Jo Mackie, and all others working hard to defend, restore and rewild our world–E.H.

For my illustration supporter and best friend, Tor–E.B.

First Published in 2024 by Wide Eyed Editions,
an imprint of The Quarto Group.
100 Cummings Center, Suite 265D, Beverly, MA 01915 USA.
T +1 978-282-9590 F +1 978-283-2742 www.QuartoKnows.com.

A CIP record for this book is available from the Library of Congress.

ISBN 978-0-7112-8696-2
eISBN 978-0-7112-8697-9

The illustrations are made on hot press watercolour paper, with layers of high-flow acrylic paint, watercolours and coloured pencils.
Set in Fields, Wisely, Bookmania, and Neuzeit Grotesk

Senior Commissioning Editor: Lucy Brownridge
Designer: Sasha Moxon
Production Controller: Dawn Cameron
Art Director: Karissa Santos
Publisher: Debbie Foy

Manufactured in Guangdong, China TT122023
9 8 7 6 5 4 3 2 1

MIX
Paper | Supporting
responsible forestry
FSC® C016973
www.fsc.org

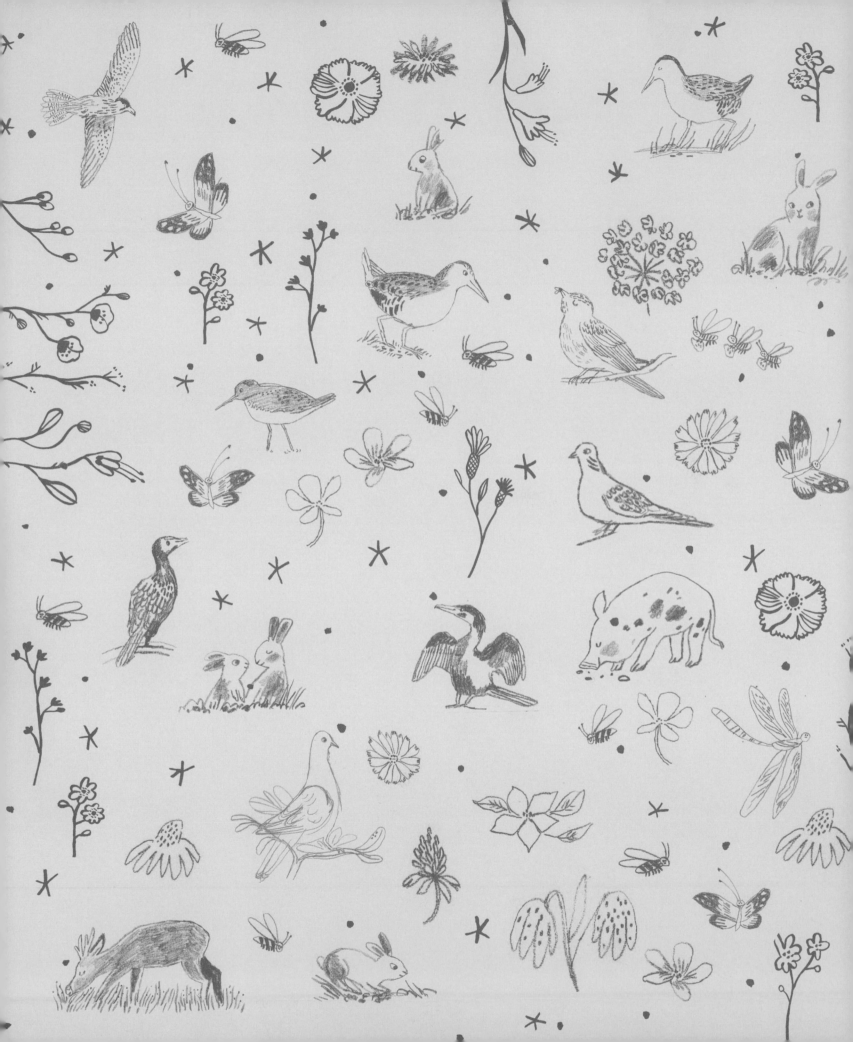